Table of Contents

Life in the Trees

Howler monkeys are some of the loudest animals on land. Their deep howls fill the rain forests of South America.

World Map

North America

Europe

Asia

Africa

South America

Australia

Antarctica

South America has 13 kinds of howler monkeys. They spend most of their time in the trees. They live in troops of three to 20 monkeys.

South America Map

where howler monkeys live

Up Close!

Howler monkeys have red, black, gold, or brown hair. They weigh up to 25 pounds (11 kilograms). Males are larger than females.

Howler monkey tails can reach 3 feet (0.9 meter) long. These monkeys use their tails like an anchor. Their tails grip branches while they sleep.

Finding Food

In the treetops howler monkeys
eat shoots and leaves.
They munch on flowers,
fruit, and insects.

Howler monkeys look for water
in the trees. They touch wet
leaves and lick the water off
their hands. They drink
from streams and ponds too.

Growing Up

Females give birth to one baby
at a time. Babies ride on their
mothers' backs for about a year.
In the wild, howlers live
up to 25 years.

Staying Safe

Harpy eagles hunt young howlers. To keep their young safe, troop members keep watch. They howl if danger is near.

Howlers find food and safety in
the trees. But rain forests are
in danger. People are trying to
save rain forests so howlers
always have a place to live.

Glossary

anchor—an object that holds something in place

harpy eagle—one of the world's largest and most powerful eagles; it is found in the rain forests of Central and South America

howl—to make a loud, sad noise; howler monkeys howl to warn others in their troop and to mark their territory in the trees

rain forest—a thick forest where a great deal of rain falls

shoot—the white stem growing out of a seed that becomes a plant

troop—a group

Read More

Ganeri, Anita. *Howler Monkey*. A Day in the Life. Rain Forest Animals. Chicago: Heinemann Library, 2011.

Gosman, Gillian. *Howler Monkeys*. Monkey Business. New York: PowerKids Press, 2012.

Lunis, Natalie. *Howler Monkey: Super Loud*. Animal Loudmouths. New York: Bearport, 2012.

Internet Sites

FactHound offers a safe, fun way to find Internet sites related to this book. All of the sites on FactHound have been researched by our staff.

Here's all you do:

Visit *www.facthound.com*

Type in this code: 9781429675895

Super-cool stuff! Check out projects, games and lots more at www.capstonekids.com

Index

Word Count: 212
Grade: 1
Early-Intervention Level: 17